v/uy

Insects

BY ALLAN MOREY

amicus
high interest

Amicus High Interest is an imprint of Amicus
P.O. Box 1329, Mankato, MN 56002
www.amicuspublishing.us

Library of Congress Cataloging-in-Publication Data
Morey, Allan, author.
 Insects / Allan Morey.
     pages cm. – (Animal kingdom)
Summary: "An introduction to what characteristics insects
have and how they fit into the animal kingdom"
—Provided by publisher.
Audience: Grade K to 3.
 Includes bibliographical references and index.
 ISBN 978-1-60753-474-7 (library binding) –
 ISBN 978-1-60753-621-5 (ebook)
1. Insects–Juvenile literature. I. Title.
QL467.2.M67 2015
595.7–dc23

                                        2013031902

Editor: Wendy Dieker
Series Designer: Kathleen Petelinsek
Book Designer: Heather Dreisbach
Photo Researcher: Kurtis Kinneman

Photo Credits: Arvind Balaraman / Shutterstock cover; NHPA
/ SuperStock 5; Steve Anderson / Alamy 6; Zen Shui /
SuperStock 9; Biosphoto / SuperStock 10; Martin Shields /
Alamy 13; blickwinkel / Alamy 14; Lon Brehmer and Enriqueta
Flores-Guevara 17; Christian GUY / imagebr / imagebroker.
net / SuperStock 18; Universal Images Group / SuperStock
20; Biosphoto / SuperStock 23; PhotoStock-Israel / Alamy
25; Antje Schulte - Insects / Alamy 26; Markus Hermenau /
Westend61 / SuperStock 29

Printed in the United States of America at Corporate Graphics
in North Mankato, Minnesota.

10 9 8 7 6 5 4 3 2 1

Table of Contents

What Is an Insect?

An ant is an insect. So is a grasshopper and a moth. How are they alike? Count their legs. Adult insects have six. That's more than birds, lizards, or mice. Spiders and ticks creep around on eight legs. So they're not insects either. But beetles, cockroaches, and water bugs are.

 How many kinds of insects are there?

A flower beetle crawls around on six legs. It is an insect.

 So far, scientists have discovered about one million. They are finding more every day.

This beetle has three
body sections.

 Q What are **antennae** used for?

While looking at a butterfly or a bee, also count its body parts. How many do you see? Adult insects have three main parts. They have a head. That's where their mouth, eyes, and antennae are. Six legs poke out of their thorax, or middle. Their tail end is called an abdomen.

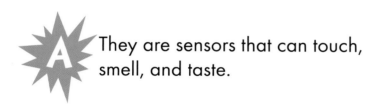

They are sensors that can touch, smell, and taste.

Adult insects have an **exoskeleton**. This outer shell serves as armor. It protects their soft bodies.

Most insects can fly. Just look at mosquitoes, wasps, and dragonflies. Even beetles flitter about. Beetles have a pair of hard outer wings. Hidden under them, they have a set of soft wings. They use the soft wings to fly.

An insect sheds its hard exoskeleton.

9

This beetle eats flower petals.

Eat or Be Eaten

What do insects eat? Just about anything. They munch on plants and animals. Some even eat trash!

Insects have many ways to get food. Locusts, butterflies, and aphids all eat plants. Locusts chew on leaves with powerful jaws. Butterflies suck up nectar with tube-like mouths. Tiny aphids have needle-like mouthparts. They poke them into plants to feed.

Some insects are **predators**. Praying mantises snatch up other insects with powerful front legs. Large water bugs swim under the water to catch small fish and frogs.

Still other insects are **parasites**. Mosquitoes and fleas bite animals. Then they suck up the animals' blood. Lice feed on the skin, blood, and feathers of animals.

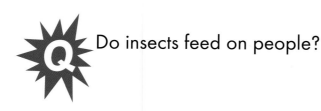Do insects feed on people?

A water strider is a predator. It makes a meal of another insect.

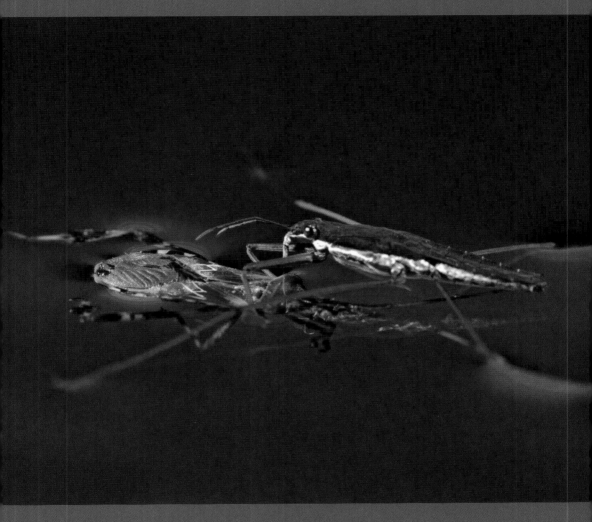

Mosquitoes do. So do some flies, fleas, and lice. Bed bugs bite people while they sleep.

**This Venus flytrap caught
a bug to eat.**

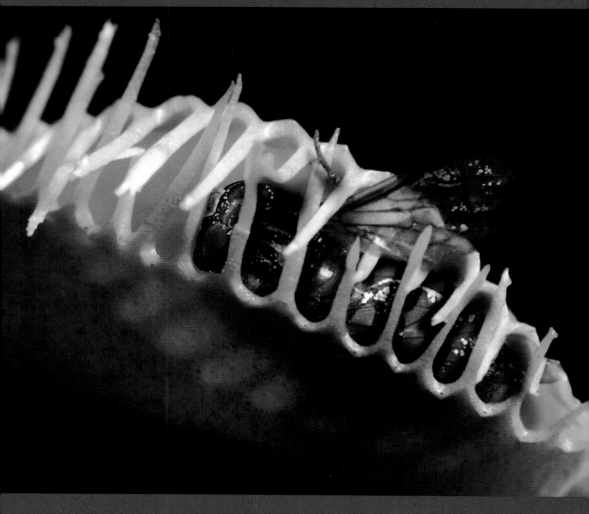

 Do people eat insects?

What eats insects? Just about every type of animal. They are food for many birds. Bats, lizards, snakes, frogs, fish, and mice also eat insects. Even some plants do!

Luckily, insects have ways to protect themselves. Some moths look like tree bark. Their **camouflage** makes it hard to spot them. Wasps have stingers. Ants have pincers. And stink bugs just smell too bad to eat.

 Yes. In South America, some people fry up ants. They snack on them like popcorn.

Where Do Insects Live?

Insects live almost everywhere. Insects are found wherever there is food. This includes treetops and ponds. They can live in caves and under the ground. Insects are found in people's homes and trash.

Insects can live in harsh habitats. Ironclad beetles need little water. They live in dry deserts. Arctic beetles are hardy enough to survive in snow and ice.

An ironclad beetle survives
in the dry desert.

Honeybees live in colonies and work together to make honey.

 Q How large can insect **colonies** get?

Some insects live in colonies. They work as a team to gather food. Leafcutter ants cut up large leaves. They carry the pieces back to their nests to make food.

Colonies also protect their hives. If a hornet nest is bothered, angry hornets swarm out. They may sting any animals that get too close to their hive.

 Some hornet and wasp colonies may have hundreds insects. Ant colonies can number in the thousands.

This butterfly lays eggs on a leaf. The babies will eat the leaves when they hatch.

Metamorphosis

After mating, a female insect lays her eggs. She may bury them in the ground. Some females may place them on a plant. Others will even put them inside a dead animal. The eggs just need to be near food. Young insects are very hungry when they hatch. They are called **larvae**. Many larvae are too small to find food on their own.

Some larvae are very different than adult insects. They look like worms. You'd call them caterpillars or grubs. Others look a lot like adults. They are just smaller and don't have wings.

Young insects eat and eat to grow quickly. A larva may go from a tiny speck to a fat caterpillar in weeks.

Some insects look like tiny
adults when they hatch.

All larvae go through a change called **metamorphosis**. For some insects, they just get bigger and grow wings. But butterflies, beetles, and bees are different. They go through a **pupa** stage. They wrap themselves in a **cocoon**. Their bodies change. They grow legs and wings. When they burst out, they are adult insects.

This butterfly is ready to come out of its cocoon.

A bee spreads pollen from flower to flower as it eats nectar.

 Can insects harm people?

Insects in the World

Many people think insects are pests. They bite. They sting. But every animal has a purpose. When a bee lands on a flower, pollen gets trapped on its hairy legs. The bee then buzzes off. It spreads pollen to other plants. These plants need the pollen to make seeds.

 Most can't. But some insects, like mosquitoes, carry diseases. They can infect a person with a bite.

Insects are nature's garbage collectors. Roll over a fallen tree. Underneath, there will be all sorts of hungry critters. You might find ants, beetles, and even some grubs. Insects clean up nature. They eat dead animals, fallen trees and leaves, and animal waste.

You many not always like insects. They can be pests. But they have important jobs to do.

**Wasps eat fallen fruit
before it rots.**

Glossary

antenna A feeler; some insects use their antennae to touch, smell, taste, and even hear.

camouflage Coloring that makes insects look like their surroundings.

cocoon A protective covering a larva makes to live in during metamorphosis.

colony A group of animals that live and work together to find food and shelter.

exoskeleton A hard outer shell.

larvae A young insect.

metamorphosis The process in which young insects change into adults.

parasite An animal, such as a bed bug or flea, that feeds off of another animal.

predator An animal that hunts other animals for food.

pupa An insect in the stage between larvae and adult.

Read More

Gray, Susan H. *The Life Cycle of Insects.* Chicago: Heinemann Library, 2012.

Shea, Nicole. *Creepy Bugs.* New York: Gareth Stevens Publishing, 2012.

Stein, Peter. *Bugs Galore.* Somerville, MA: Candlewick Press, 2012.

Websites

Bug Pictures—National Geographic Kids
http://kids.nationalgeographic.com/kids/photos/bugs/

Pest World for Kids
http://www.pestworldforkids.org/guide.html

San Diego Zoo Kids—Arthropods
http://kids.sandiegozoo.org/animals/insects

Index

About the Author

Allan Morey grew up on a farm in central Wisconsin, where he had a pet pig named Pete. Allan's early love of animals has stayed with him his entire life. He's had pet fish, mice, gerbils, cockatiels, cats, and even a ferret. Currently, his dog, Ty, is curled up by his feet while he writes.